# Cold Mountain and The Sea

ALSO BY BARRY HILL

*The Schools* (1977)
*A Rim of Blue: Stories* (1978)
*Near the Refinery: a novella* (1980)
*Headlocks and Other Stories* (1983)
*The Best Picture: a novel* (1988)
*Raft: Poems 1983–1990* (1990)
*Sitting In* (1991)
*Ghosting William Buckley: a poem* (1993)
*The Rock: Travelling to Uluru* (1997)
*The Inland Sea: Poems* (2001)
*Broken Song: T G H Strehlow and Aboriginal Possession* (2002)
*The Enduring Rip: A History of Queenscliffe* (2004)
*The War Sonnets* (2007)
*Necessity: Poems 1996–2006* (2007)
*Four Lines East* (2007)
*As We Draw Ourselves* (2008)
*Lines for Birds* (2011)
*Naked Clay: Drawing from Lucian Freud* (2012)
*Peacemongers* (2014)
*Grass Hut Work* (2016)
*Reason & Lovelessness: Essays, encounters, reviews 1980–2017* (2018)
*Eagerly We Burn: Selected Poems: 1980–2018* (2019)
*Kind Fire* (2020)

# Cold Mountain and The Sea

Barry Hill

ARCADIA

First published 2021 by ARCADIA
*the general books' imprint of*
Australian Scholarly Publishing Pty Ltd
7 Lt Lothian St Nth, North Melbourne, Victoria 3051

*tel* 03 9329 6963 / *fax* 03 9329 5452
aspic@ozemail.com.au / www.scholarly.info

ISBN: 978-1-922669-25-4



*Book design:* Joe Hill
*Cover photograph:* Getty Images

*for my mother, Mavis Hill, 1918–1981*

*It is very probable that at a good distance from the Shore there exists a Channel of deeper Water round the Edge of this Sand Bank and this point shall not be left undetermined.*

JOHN MURRAY, The Summer Survey, Log of the *Lady Nelson*, March, 4 1802, approaching the sandy cliffs at the heads of Port Phillip Bay.

*The Tao drifts*
*It can go left or right*

LAO TZU

*The water gouges the cliff*
*and pounds the rocks unceasingly.*

*Even from a distance we know how high it is.*

*How can the valley stream be blocked?*
*It will end up in the ocean as billows.*

ZEN MASTER DOGEN

*Above Cold Mountain's peak, the moon's lone disc*
*illuminates the clear sky—nothing else appears.*
*Honour this priceless natural treasure*
*hidden in the five streams of your drowning body.*

HAN SHAN (Cold Mountain)

# CONTENTS

## 2 A Night Of Serious Drinking With Han Shan

## 3 Dark Pearl

# 1 Shaman Late In The Day

# Spawn

A warm blue sea
drew a glossy beautiful woman
into itself—a shaman late in the day.
She had the outgoing tide to herself.

She swam towards the horizon
as if to leave her spawning place.
She went at a clip—pool-trained
her elbows a little too high, like fins.

I bowed to her last Xmas Eve
when she stepped down from the pulpit
having recited some lines of her own
that matched her beauty

complimenting the Nativity
by reference to a newborn
the fourth of her children, her latest hymn.
Only a demon would query her glow.

So you like poetry? I said
as we happened to stand
side by side outside the chapel (which is not my own
though sometimes I go, for 'poetic' reasons).

Oh yes, she said, and climbed into the old family van.
This evening, she rode her bike to the sea.
Her hair in a bun, her goggles pink.
The flippers went on when she was calf-deep.

She had the legs of a runner.
Her swimsuit offered a moon view
slice of buttock, white as abalone.
And she set off, free

O so free of her off-spring
and the devoted one, the sweet husband.
With the first stroke she claimed the open water.
I watched her divorce and abandon

everything and everyone to her own
self-alone in the shark-infested sea.
Except that nothing is infested, not really.
It is what it is, as they say, moronically.

As I write, dusk is falling.

## What I Thought I Knew

Last year, a friend, a former
Bishop as it happens
sent me season's greetings:
that I find nativity within
a place in my heart
to be newborn—
a native to the best
that life can be and become.

I would thank him from
the rag and bone bottom
of whatever it is, these days
that makes me angry, sad, ill.
But my heart's wish was to erase
error, along with my good
self if needs be

with these finely tuned
co-morbidities. Yes, I recently said
to a dying friend
it will be an honor to write
your obituary, I will—
but preferably without signing;
some books improve without names.

Some say I should do
another 'bird book'— as refuge.
Work on the feathers, night calls
the habits of cuckoos
carry on being what an aboriginal
elder once grinningly said I was:
Number One Emu.

There are dances out there.
Squatting in the silence.
There are secret names
in noisy bird songs.
It's not masking that gives
*persona* its grit—

It's the blazing wind…

These were some
of the ten thousand things
I thought I knew back then.

## Low Tide, Flying Start

The wind is gentle and in the east.
It keeps the ocean-fresh southerly at bay.
It's ideal for warm slack water
soundless naming.

On the new day of the year
you write out the first verse
of the *Tao Te Ching.*
*Te* is supposed to mean *integrity*
(even when you're wrong!)

That's fine, that's as good as it gets.
What's your resolution, dear old self?
'Dear' as in bloodied
by the rusty star picket you stepped upon
gathering sweet basil on Xmas Eve.

'Dear' as in time unfolding
in *Emergency* on Xmas Eve.
Dear as delicate and paper-thin
skin that resists stitching
(like my old man's at my age).

And what about that kid on his dad's knee
offering his bloody index finger
to the Triage nurse. That was fine, too.
Less so the elderly drunken woman
leaning on a friend's bony shoulder.

You had a young doctor
an Irishman with a streaming cold
who put a mask on after you asked.
Sure, he said, sure, don't mind me if I do.
And called a nurse to do the stitching.

You got out of there at midnight.
No need to wish anybody a silly Merry Xmas.
Nor did you have to wipe
the scummy tables at Maccas:
you ate in the car—

drove home with the roof open.
That was fresh enough
almost nameless enough
good fortune enough
getting home stitched up

in the wee hours.

## Day 1: Early Kill

It was still damp and
so tiny you could miss it
in the thin pile of carpet on the stairs.

Its snout was the thing.
A single-pointed end
its eyes moist

its body wet, I supposed
from the mouthing Wally gave it
before curling to sleep
at the feet of our beloved.

What to call a stain
in a half-used tissue?
Blood from the gullet
perforated by cat-passion—

a smear on the floor
aftermath like an afterthought
of a name (Wally after Whitman
I am pleased to say).

Now it's in the bin with nothing
to its name. I have
the whole day ahead of me.
What to do?

I'll copy another set of Picasso etchings.
That is what I'll do.
Let my beloved sleep on.
Let her be as naked as the Model

gazing at the Sculptor
as the carving faces her
heart-shaped face, the half
moons of her tender eyes

as she lies
in the arms of her man—
him that is hers
and her that is his.

Look at Wally now.
He sleeps with brother Rumi.
Their dozing renders them indistinguishable.
Together they make a cello.

The sleeping sounds are made of fur.
They are as harmless
as fur-balls, and with all
this trusty sleeping going on

it might be a good year
or if not a blessed one—
but I go too far:
I will just find where I am

on the stairs of experience
when experience is
my unspoken name.
Boy, what a year this could be!

## Day 8: Change

(Don't ask me
what happened to the other days).
I'm already skipping pages in the diary.
Hoping I can write the next line

with the finesse
of a character rendered
with right breath, spinal strength
posture roped by the radicals…

But what a novice annunciator
I am; archaic word pictures confound me—
yet effort is not lacking
the surf rolls in at the Heads

I can see the new weather coming
from low in the south-west
to close the furnace door
blasting from the north.

The heat lasts for days.
Funny though—
I seldom get back to the sea
before the change.

One minute, it's an immortal
bolt of cloth, infinite satin.
Next it's ripple and chop.
I dive into a lament of bad timing.

# Day 9: Breakfast

As you managed to write out in Chinese—
*Heaven and Earth are heartless*
*Treating creatures like straw dogs.*

Not so much because you feel it so today
not counting tomorrow
or the day after that in the new year

but just as much because
you like the look
of the characters

especially the signs for
*Heaven and Earth.*
*Straw Dogs*

were not made for love
but sacrifice: they were bound
for festive occasions, trussed up

to be hurled into the street
or the backwash of calamity—
rags everywhere, reduced to being

as slow-moving as stingrays.
Actually, the stingray at my swimming spot
is as wide as a breakfast tray:

I swam over it in fright.
I felt our hearts miss a beat.
My character for mutual heroism

would have to hint at being
languid and eluding nets of names
fatty though they be.

## Day 13: Damage On The Path

The idea of a bike's front wheel
mounting your coccyx
scaling your discs
without so much
as the tinkling of a bell!

Goes to show
the intrepid nature
of your outing
along the blackstone wall
and the gift you're developing

in swallowing anger
at the world's lack of warning—
You typed *warming*—
another accident
as happens in poems.

The cold facts are:
on the ordinary path
and out there
where the mackerel sea
turns ultramarine

and the indigo is
as deep as the reef
there's no warning
from here to there
swim as you might.

## Two Pre-Christmas Poems

### **Pneumonia Meal**

A wholemeal wife
with a Lutheran aura
hovering over the bench
thickening and lightening the light.

A woman cake-baking for Christmas
filling the kitchen with sweet forms
batches of perfectly timed goodness
happier than she can say:

that her ailing husband is resting
asleep upstairs with the cats
that he's hardly stirred on discovering
that he still lives, albeit

with a dry mouth, a thirst
yet breathing coming good
with an absence of blood
he can walk down the stairs following his nose

to stand in the kitchen
tempted to lick the sweat
of her brow, her upper lip.
But she's too hot to embrace

it would not be a favour
just let her be in the aroma
of shortbread, the sugar-dust glistening
a singe in the air of caramel undersides.

A woman of biscuity warmth
    not wanting his tongue
        so much as his mouth
open for the golden produce, his smiling into munch…

And later, after his palette swam
    of almond meal
        the juice in his mouth
reminded him of being young

when his mother raided her purse
    to lash out on the fillet steak—
        which she cooked rare, scarlet
his first meal home from hospital.

## After Kissing Her Throat Slowly Without Coughing

And this year
look what she's made you do:
After looking around the garden
not counting so much as
devouring with your older eyes

flower after flower she has planted
now in pre-Christmas bloom
not for you, no, not for you
but for the garden's sake—
and in honor of the golden-leafed tree

spread-eagled in blue air
announcing itself again
as you were driven to do
something of the same:
ask for a Christmas gift, when not even a Christian

when all you aspire to be
is an uncarved block—
a do-nothing man in harmlessness
a do-nothing and ask-nothing
kind of person, if person you be…

You want a ring, a wedding ring now!
A wedding ring now, she cried
after all this time?
But she'd lit up, hiding a smile.
It would be her pleasure, she crooned, her pleasure.

After jotting this in happy pathos
you remember those times
when your new wife had to break open
with laughter, there was no faking it with this guy—
spreading herself like a tree fully glowing.

## Blue Eyes

More reading won't make a difference.
An early love, David Herbert Lawrence, knew that.

With degrees of hope, he reached the Antipodes
only to get dumped by a wave on its ocean shore.

Thank *Revelations* he survived, and is still with you.
He swam in fire, flew with eagles

knew which breast his love was buttered on.
Division, yes, but no confusion!

Maybe, before going up or under yourself
you can make a pyre of his exclamations—

let them become cinders, trust his carbon traces.
And shut up shop with the poetry caper.

Make as if becalmed as you look out to sea
scanning for burning decks.

Along this coast many a ship went down:
fellow citizens of old, watched from the sandy cliffs

as women and children drowned...
Burn the books! Let co-morbidities sink

to the depths of your Unborn self.
Leave David Herbert be to dive

deeply into the blues of his dying mother's eyes.
*Life is death, and death is a kind of life.*

He might well have read this trueness
in Holderlin's German, *In Lovely Blueness.*

# Indigo

I went down to the sea on this hot hot day
me and my breathing to swim there.

I was greeted by Indigo waiting
her body along the horizon
just below the limits of my view.

The real darkness was closer—
beneath the Ultramarine
glittering beneath the fishing boats.

One boat was canopied. It seemed to have
silhouettes of mourners with their backs to me.
I hoped they'd thrown the undersized back into the water.

A shoal of Aqua was closer in
the other side of a feeble shore break
beyond which I slipped in to swim as strongly as I could.

It was perilously easy.
I was swept along by the warm northerly and
outgoing current before lifting my head

when all of a sudden something finished
my course. It was an outwash
a swathe of quick water that would have me in it.

Hello hello hello, I said to the undercurrent of Indigo.
I had stopped just short of her taking me out and down.
O another summer is here, I thought, floating on lucky stars.

I should have known. Below me—
Seaweed clumps like clouds tumbled across
the ribs of day-lit sands in *absolute roaming...*

There are days when the sea is so clear
it defines itself invisibly. No names.
No beginnings and no ends in darkness.

## Day 15: Watering

A small thing to notice:
our water pressure is best at night.
Your thirsty petalled friends
sprout and flower with gratitude
that you tend them so.

This morning
before the sun could bake them
they were patient in prayer:
you would hardly know
the depth of their relief.

And as things are, the gentlest
words I use for you, our gardener
are like the murmuring of vowels
you sing in *Petrichor*
the song that honors the ground

and brings up the essence
of perfume arising
when rain bites the dust
with sprays of consonants—
as if from sprightly words

in a perfect poem—
one that wants to go on
doing no harm to anyone.
Look at our garden sprinkler now
pulsing away under blue plums.

## Day 16: Say It Now

Because you are not going
to be able to say it too often
if again, at all—
the saying undoes it
that's the truth:

a few people confess
but no one quite knows
what to say to the truth
let alone what to do with it
when all words do

all the figures show
even the classiest
in sets of brackets
the ones you last glimpsed
the far side of Jupiter

which is obnoxiously close
pornographic in its simplicity…
The truth is
the matter to hand and
the matter that is far off

the matter between us
the matter in mind
the matter in what is said
in what the poem intimates
if the words Startrek...

around the dark matter
of which we know
next to nothing
or as good as next to.
I don't want to give the stats

you'd think the proposition false.
Best lie down and chew on it.
Chew on it as hard
as a skull to rest
your sleeping head upon.

## Day 17: Low In The Water

The weather won't budge.

Overnight, it shed
moisture on the lawn
and later this morning
a mist billowed in from the sea—
incessantly, like gentle surf
across a shark grey, fine chop.

And then, when you dived in
the first strokes took you
into the ice box
came from somewhere deep.
From beneath the thin surface.
you eddy into winter.

It's been like that all day:
small leaps of season.
Only the diehards went in
the rest stood knee-deep in shallows
looking towards the horizon
the powder blue container ship

low in the water—
faintly petrochemical.

## Day 23: Tomorrow

The kids are coming down
to Sandy Cliff
where they were born.

Childless, as yet
but still they are heading
this way to see their dad
before his teeth fall out.

What will we cook for them?
What will they like this time?
Will they let me
wake them at moon-rise
full of dark enigma?

Unborn, that's the teaching.
If they let me
I'll tell them about them
being unborn.
Oh, I hear them yawn—

I do believe they hardly want
to know the details
of my will.
They have had
enough of my will!

More enlightenment!

## Day 25: Founding Fathers

All night the wind is in the north.
Gaining speed
blowing though the room
like a train, the curtains, the bellows.

Up north—no monsoon rain.
A phalanx of heat squats
on the burnt continent
making of it an empty

convict settlement.
All this confounded weather talk
puts us in chains.
What is there to celebrate

but the fires along the horizon
smoke drifting
across the water—
smoke without signaling.

Get out of the house now.
Quick, before it goes up.
*The Tao makes no claims*
*Has no desires.*

## Day 26: Potato Salad

Will be made this evening
by your beloved
when the change comes.

She would have showered.
The cats will emerge from their attic
among the clean towels.

Slinking around her feet
full of Dark Virtue
they create the climate

and they know it.
*Dark Virtue goes deep*
*goes far, goes the other way*

said Master Lao.
*Until it reaches perfect harmony.*

They were the days.

## All Muzzle

Call it Plum Rain.
It sweetens growth.
You can see the beans climbing.

Wally came in wet
and alarmed. I dried him off
and he munched chicken necks.

Now he's upstairs snoring, side by side
with his mate and my mate.
Her lips would be slightly apart.

Their faces are all muzzle, eyes shut.
In Paradise everyone has fine whiskers.
Ensemble of snores to be heard above the rain

that becalms the sea
with its pock pock to the far horizon
it's little disturbances disappearing

like the gannet high above me yesterday.
It must have taken its flutter and dive
elsewhere. I bet it's retreated

to the rookery called Pope's Eye
walled up in World Thoughtfulness
further out than the seals.

## Survival

Today the water lapped for you.
And you would not come.
The illuminated swathe of mackerel green
was inviting, but you could not go in.

Your body in strange and distant mourning.
The beach stretched from dune to dune.
The dogs, in friendly fashion, bound towards
and then around you. Doleful eyes.

Out there, only a ball-for-a dog-away
the reef fish were swimming in shadows
the gold and the bronze fading
as they slide away, slide away.

Endure, says a voice on the breeze.
Live without saying too much.
Think of your head on a faithless shoulder
your cheek against a warm throat.

O you can look up and speak, as you must.
You have to say the essential things.
We are damned when we do not.
Risk glibness, and bathos, —

be as soundless as an ocean trout.

## Approaching Father's Day, 2020

The doves are back in the garden.

Sitting on the clothes line
that does not have any clothes on.

They plump up, shift plump weights
as simply together as can be.

As if they are happy infinitely
in their domestic lockdown.

A wattle-bird shoots in
out of the blue.

I get a flash
of its fleshy redneck

its squawk obliterates coos
and the doves are gone.

Shows what peace is made of.

Now the signs are clear:
everyone is gearing up

for the next stage
whatever it may be—

a free-for-all?
A contagious pall of nurses?

There's a female maggie
at the door

eye-balling me
near the cat's bowl.

What a decision to have to make.
O poor I am in myself

as Mista Crow arrives
with his shroud.

There's no escaping—
every choice a mortal one.

## Not Forgotten By

Currawong high in Mahogany gum
parrots in the lower reaches, grubby
Ibis zoning back from the garbage dump
Doves canoodling in olives, bats
in eves near the Pecan, rusty leaves
in the moon's rise, bright bright

virtue becoming clear, pale
eggshell blues, creamy silver
a cloud arisen with edges, cobalt evening dress
the land darkened before, below
and still the shimmer, the trembling
lamp drawing itself up—ice fire.

Fire and ice. Who said that? What exactly?
*On the other side of brightness*
*the Chinese have landed.*
Don't say a word, words burn out.
Words have nothing to do with it.
Words are for the birds.

There's no getting close
when rising is all around us
in us when bearing to see the unborn
the one before us rising
to fall out of the sky
into seething sea.

# Scaled

The heat is back.
Again you'll swim as far as you can.

You'll go in where it's clear and the depth uncertain.
You'll swim with a view of the shadowy bottom
the gutters and grit of the new debris.

Half way along—your marker's a high
white triangle up on the dune—
you'll tire at the benign tide

running out. It will *stay you*
check your progress, if you seek to call it that.
You might think 'flounder'

though it was no such thing.
What you saw was a silver pause
a glittering school in a watery sky.

Who can deny the progress
of whitebait in the then and the now
and the what is to be?

You float awhile.
It is the clear light that holds you
a flickering that vanishes at a glance.

Life goes by in a silver shoal.
You turn to swim the home-going length
of the black stone wall

as a backwash swells with its utmost strength
seeking to take you further out.

## Summer Almost Over, Peace Talks Far Off

The sea so clear you didn't mind
the early chill. You loved its
nip of winter under the belt.

And the lazy fish below, fat salmon
the colour of pewter, their fins yellow
bronze near the gills.

You swam at odd angles: too much kelp.
You were not thinking, just swimming
and still breathing to the best

of venerable skill.
What were you trying to expel?
What was being exhaled in the cooling sea?

You were refusing to say, you were sticking
to your guns in some armory of a bay—
still exhaling thoughts of Peace Talks

not to mention the acrid air
of bushfires, trying to keep fatalities
from front of mind, you were treading

water in grief
albeit for the far side of your world.
How vigorously you dried yourself!

Toweling yourself down, balls and all
kicking the togs off
standing naked on the bitumen

as if the enemy was miles off.

## Water Deeper Than

A baking sun walks you into the sea.

Do not fear a thing.

The sea offers such clear feeling—
        like having a loving hand
                in the small of your back.

Before you know it you are in
        arms-around, beyond sex
                with the loins wet.

Yesterday you swam swiftly beyond the others.
        The holiday crowd stood
                as if with their masks on.

You were just a little further out, treading
        water deeper than yourself
                while they kept their shoulders warm.

The ray below you must have known that.
        He-she spread its huge tablecloth
                in the cloudy sand

flapped in the sea-sky, climbed again
        into clarity with a touch of aqua—
                no threat to anybody

if anybody were to notice
        how close he-she was
                in dangerous languid motion.

When she vanished eastwards
        you swam in the same same direction—
                and found her again, dancing Swan Lake.

## Filthy

Today a small one glided across my way.
Or was it the same as the other day—

the big one when younger
as I am weaker and older?

Hard to tell with the sea.
It can age you like the shore.

It makes you older and younger
at the same time, often the same day.

The next visit is easier to describe:
the water was filthy with weed

heavy with sand and cloud.
I'd left it too late in the day.

Even the scum looked cold
the waves arrived in grubby rolls

filthy roll on filthy roll.
I squibbed it, offended the day

and the ray.
We've come this far, my father used to say

before diving in, striking out.
Without him now, hardly older

than he was then
I'm sad when I let him down.

## Nowhere To Go

No one renders a lingering plague in the sea.
No one has caught the fullness of a wave mutating.

They carry on about the rise in sea-levels
without a thought for the metastasis of waters gestating.

Sickening times, when we cling to a vision of heroes
and their beautiful wives with perfectly false eyelashes

calling for vodka to share with their doomed husbands.
It's enough to make you want to shit in a Moscow cathedral.

Oh, I know, there's injustice all over the world.
There is a limit to what we can do! Except be hopeful.

Like the people in Sudan, for instance, or Idlib.
I have, I confess, lost track of my own disgusting neglect.

Nowhere to go. Even when I swim straight
out from the shore through the filth of a day

I take in the cold as if I was the one
growing old in Belmarsh—eating optimism like bitterness

flogging myself for whatever his incarceration is becoming.
Why, only yesterday, walking past a young Life Guard

I had to put on a face of gratitude
for the volunteerism, the vacant eyes, puppy cheeks.

## Surfer's Ear

I'd been to the doctor for being half deaf
with surfer's ear that set in as a boy—
not scummy wax so much as the sea itself
trapped by swollen bones near the drum.

I got to the beach by noon, at low-tide
little having been done at the clinic.
Yet the sea was as inviting as a gentle nurse.
I walked slowly into serenity plus

and swam out with the tide against me
the water clear all the way to the bottom.
It is good to swim hard and get almost
nowhere. The sea is a lesson

in calm, in reality, in welcome, in emptiness
of will, in the way forward when
forward is not the point: days when it pays
to be deaf and dumb to the world.

## Not To Worry

These hesitations in the shallows
of flat grey icy water
are not failures
at the change of season
they are registrations of the wild
grammar of swimming:

legs might freeze
cock and balls come to little
when all that's happening
is that you are going to plunge
into the sea, come what may.

Anyway, your hair's silver now
comorbidities are snug as bugs in a rug.
With that in mind, take your dive
laugh that it might be your last
strike out parallel with the indigo reef

at the edge of which you once
spotted the butterfish which
with a flick of its juicy tail
made a muscular turn
above Mother Ray

still lucid above
bank on bank of sandy ribs—
so defined you'd think the seabed
was staring up at it, and at you,
you with your breathy greeting poems.

# 2 A Night Of Serious Drinking With Han Shan

*Eighty years ago I was born into the world.*
*A thousand, ten thousand miles I've roamed*

*by rivers where the grass is lush*
*beyond the border where the red earth blows.*

*I brewed potions in a vain quest to defeat death.*
*I read books, I sang songs of history.*

*And today I've come home to Sandy Cliff*
*to drown my face in surf and wash my ears*
*to rinse my mouth with a stone and polish my teeth.*

HAN SHAN

## Petty Recoveries, Shamanic Nose Dives

After not going into the sea
not braving the cold water
in the brusque southerly
*squidding* it, one might say.

Instead, he watches the video
of the great Grand Final that ended
drawn. The huge, healthy crowd seethed
at the thought of traipsing back *en masse.*

Next week, after Easter
it could be worse, if push comes to shove.
He must endure a rebirth in the wintery straits
foaming with mutations of virus...

His own borders closing, is that the feeling?
Not constricted breathing so much
as a thickening of humbug in congregations
a spewing of make-believe in the *polis.*

It's beyond a joke. It is *all* Dark Learning:
spasms of Tao in the Warring States Period:
poems that stick in the throat
prose that ends in swamps:

no long flights today, ladies and gentleman.
(this way to the gas, said the violinist).
No divinity in womanly eyes.
No ashes of the mind needed more than now.

Cast about for the warm things.
Try not to slide off the ox.
Leave behind the Keeper of the Pass.
Remember this: you barely existed.

## I Woke To A Full Moon

The first night after
he'd been driving me around and around.

Our first drink was poured in the dark.
Soon, all I could see were the empties.

Before dawn I found a lamp post
swung off it to see

my reflections in a puddle.
Useless.

Han Shan accused me of impatience.
He gave me a tide chart, and laughed.

A poet I know, a distant friend—
a serious drinker after breaking out

of his monastery
having taken an axe to the temple floor

was drinking for days before pouring
boiling oil into his ears.

He woke on the deck of a ferry
with furious ocean sounds to himself.

*Hearing. Listening.* In the Lotus Sutra
they seem inter-changeable.

Sit it out, I can hear Han Shan whispering.
Sit it out. Drink in the silence.

We were in our cups.
It was not going to end.

## Hungover With Han Shan

Now, among whispy clouds near the peak
or in cold waters
of a becalmed sea—
chilled to the bone, the body a dead weight

what's to say?
Everything must have been said.
You are *unborn*, yet to take your bearings.
When the clouds clear—the sea remains.

Your sea, here, is near the ocean.
It's the ocean winds that bring the tides in.
If you were to swim today; sanity!
And the fishy return of the old jokes.

Once you saw Bill Porter in 'Han Shan's cave'.
He was in the jaw of the opening
like an elder at Uluru.
Just a video, but a sobering one.

Each time Han Shan turns his back
wanders off from you
not saying a word
it's hard to deny his Way.

One morning, still sugared up
from the night-talk
the silent cold of the sea
is a cure, almost a balm

with all that the ocean knows:
the sweetness of reason lingers—
for the tremendous silent arousal
of submarine murmurings, octopus quiet.

## Yesterday The Sea Was So

Beautifully ultramarine
with the indigo rippling beneath
you walked in expecting
anything but stillness.

Sure enough, as hard as you swam
you made little progress
against the current and
submarine swirl.

Still, you came out
as proud as old man seal
to be among his colony
the sea pouring off him.

Dumb, Han Shan cackled.
Get a grip on yourself.
There's no future in happiness.
You know that.

## Fresh Water Memory Of Old Times

The slack water can
remind him of the rock pool
where, finally, he dropped two
wedding rings into cloudy depths—

watching them slow to the bottom
of the muddy source of things.
To think: of an old marriage
full of cake libretto—

then went deeply quiet:
it was becalmed and cursed
as if her Hitler was to blame
for his unrelenting Irishness.

It was good to let the rings go.
They sank down through the
silty waters of the gorge
where they'd *tied the knot.*

Now, down there, old man
yabbie wears one around his neck.
The other ring found the tail of a female.
The inland site remains an increase place.

Han Shan, remote from wife
and child, labours no point.
He licks rocks, steps into footprints
of tigers, once did dance with a bear.

## Han Shan Casts About In Time Of Plague

**1**

He thinks of taking flowers to people
leaving them a little bunch on their step
sauntering off to die without them knowing.

Watching them from the night trees
one by one sharing the flowers
chewing their cud, laughing.

**2**

Dread of that image. Of so many starving men
on a route march back to their villages
from where other people will banish them.

It is raining Straw Dogs.
Han Shan is becoming fit for one drum.
The drum will do him until one more end.

**3**

Do not fear, he tells them
when he summons the powers of speech.
Straw Dogs will be pulverized by us.

They are part of us, we are part of them.
We're in this together
for all of the season, until year's end.

**4**

Han Shan remembers Cold Mountain—
the place the mountain the name.
He goes looking for his cave again.

## Han Shan Does Himself Over

A firm rendition of himself in clear water—
looking down at himself, fish and jelly like.
He did his best to expunge himself.

Han Shan works hard without working hard.
He reduces himself, and reduces himself again—
an image made of dust and running water.

Han Shan made his face like nothing else.
Silly old fossil was Han Shan.
All that elbow grease for Original Face.

Along came Han Shan's mother, his father
and the children who had long forgotten him.
Snow covered everything.

Han Shan arose in his dream in the blizzard:
that he was air-born in absolute wandering—
free as a snow flake, melting all the way.

## Killing Time Drawing

This is a true story about drawing my face in a time of plague.
It is not a fake story about Cold Mountain.
It's tale of a man attacking what he can see of himself.

He is going to call it Mode of Attack, Resistance all Over.
Having given up hope of representing himself truly.
The best he can do is weigh in for all he is worth.

He dives into the turbulent rock-pool of himself.
The deep breath pays off and he makes it until Good Friday.
Let the believers be done with their death cult.

As long as his hand is touching the paper he is out of his depth.
When he lifts carbon fingers and takes stock.
He is face to face with clarifying failure. Should he keep drawing?

One kind reader will surely know.
What's this arrival in the studio? Wife
or butcher bird, only time and the song will tell.

There is a new statute on the books.
That we attend our own funerals alone.
That loved ones hoard the images.

You should see my clutch of erasers.
They're smeared with crimson, cobalt, indigo.
They have scattered over these bare boards.

## Damn His Pride

An old friend told me he swims well in cold waters.
A skull cap, rubber gloves, sometimes booties.
Only if he asks too much of himself does he tremble afterwards.

In his drinking days any distance was impossible.
His bodyheat must have fallen with the whiskey level .
Now he's on the wagon to defeat the thief the plague.

My god I envy him. I have no god and still I envy him.
An autumn hand already has me by the balls.
My balls are not much fun anymore.

Han Shan has seen everything, touched everything.
With a bear's breath, he crept up on himself and others
before curling up by the fire in the cave.

Dreaming, Cold Mountain, has seen it all.
Let us curse his diffidence, damn his pride to heaven…
But I'm not at my best today, having misplaced another eraser…

## Bodies That Float

From the depth of the cave
he can remember the first swim in very cold water
the first of the autumn tides

into which he put his leathery face
as if to wash his breath away
offering exhalations to the sandy bed

and the patches of seaweed adrift beneath him.
No, they are not stingrays.
They were the submarine clouds of reptile brains

the unborn bits and pieces he tried to imagine
in the depths of meditating on swimming
at the end of the summer.

At the end of the summer everyone is counting the dead.
Cities compete for the death count.
Cities with crowded camps disqualify themselves:

they have themselves to blame.
Han Shan is in better nick this time of year.
He strikes out for the second set of stairs.

The bodies that float bob about the buoys.
Out of puff, he rolls on his back
heaving and wheezing and calling out.

## Han Shan Up Against Himself

In quarantine, there's little to draw
he does not know too well.
He's thrown back to a cave

of hunters, wild bison men
and women with the flanks of deer
men who leave prints of their hands on walls.

Their trace is a thousand dynasties old.
Contemplating them, Han Shan feels un-carved.
He gets glimmers of himself

before the running herds
the meat is warm in his stomach
and the women in their places by the fire.

How long must Han Shan feel alone?
How to contemplate Han Shan's misery?
Must Cold Mountain be cold?

This is still the year of the plague.
Nothing falls out as it might or ought.
Even his little mates, Pick Up and Big Stick

are sounding short of breath.
They laugh, they cough, they laugh a racket
coughing falling down beside themselves.

## Difficulty Munching Night

My little mate the Inuit has nothing to say.
Lost his tongue. I can only think he has been
reading too much Han Shan.

Ezra would have called him
one of the Bamboo Grove Boys
albeit far from igloo home. *Om Muni* etc.

I know all that ice in winter would
close me down. Who needs to speak
with a mouth full of powder snow?

Munching night, how can that not
be the feeling when lingo
is out of action? But it's hard

hard not to think magically
when we think ill of our tongue.
Didn't anybody think of singing?

Pour me another and I'll go quiet.
At least give me a mask to let slip
as I give up on lost words.

## Budding

I am reading a book about how to draw naturally.
It's a classic. It first came out in America
where most of the dead are so far
surpassing all their wars.

*The impulse to draw is as natural as*
*the impulse to talk,* it begins.
It has nothing to do with aesthetics.
It is only to do with correct observation.

*And by that I mean a physical contact*
*with all sorts of objects through the senses.*
The author's name is Kiron Nicolaides.
who began by drawing contour maps for the military.

He does not say if I should learn to speak
with the naked models. But the Greek says:
*I do not care who you are.*
Each section of reading matter is fifteen hours drawing.

By my calculation I have five years drawing
ahead of me. Or behind me? An old hand already
or a novice taking one thing at a time
the ego thrown into the fire?

*If you go to a singing teacher*
*he will give you breathing exercises, not a song.*
This is the teacher I want! I start his course today
hoping he'll lead me to Han Shan.

## Shaman

Back to the easel again; what do we have here?
Your little mate from the ice and snow, the Inuit
not a half wit, even though one eye slides
off his face. Does he see in or see out?

All we know is he travelled far:
he went to the centre of the earth
kept on going, and came out afresh
on a southern icepack, paddled on a flow to here…

He has a spear in him.
It has gone right through, a barb to the left
the shaft behind him. Attacked from the rear, it seems
if he was attacked and was not showing off

what he must do to himself
to demonstrate prowess.
His sturdy stance to combat blizzards.
You drew him; now you must own him.

Fair enough.
Look at his codpiece—almost Jacobean.
And his flat feet: they are slivers in snow
like the webs of King Penguins.

## Leaving Han Shan Aside

Enough of this shilly-shallying about cold.

Bear a thought for the warm waters of teenage years
the zest of summer currents—

their fecundity, the ease of shedding
bathing suits, memories, virginity

tangy salts on sunburn, sopping paws
clumsy attempts at entry

when all you had were her arms around you
legs in and out of each others.

Nips on the neck.
The splashy truth of things.

Scratches the length of your back
as welcome as dusk—

a cover for your lingering
hard-on, the sea still warm at nightfall

and the shiver that arrives, eventually
as you walk hand in hand from the sea

loose limbed, free from the ward
of intensive care.

## True Knowledge

To put an end to mimicry
the solitary man made an effigy
of the tricky poet.

He made it with the sticks
and rags of his foul heart.
He swished his fuel

around and about, lit a match
and stepped back
just far enough so as

not to enflame himself!
A brilliant move! O
joy it was to witness

the *whoosh*
of the late poet
that motley shaman bugger

whose simple simples
are affectations best ignored—
mere predecessors to Unborn.

As the ashes
of Han Shan cool
declare your passion!

For drawings not writings
for carbon works on walls
for bison and deer

and the hand
that must be near
that sturdy surging pony

with powers of fire
water, sea and sky
thunder in its shoulders.

Now what?

# Hopeless Moon Viewing

How did my son know what to give me for Xmas?
Or what I was thinking, if thinking is the word.

This telescope will take months to assemble.
I don't have the brain for it.

My wife does, maybe she will do it, finally.
At present, I have the moon-viewing spot

with which to commune with Han Shan
and immortality.

But I don't want to go on about it
or mention the moon goddess.

On the bright nights
I'll just drag the swag onto the deck

and pretend to be in Central Australia.
Psst, I'll say to Han Shan

Get a load of this, old boy.
You don't know nothing yet.

I know I know— he will call Big Stick
who, thinking himself Manjushri

Bodhisattva of wisdom
will crack my skull

as I dream of Lake Mungo.
So much for that.

Now look at this diagram of telescope.

It is a sleeping cylinder
like a little cannon. Am I supposed

to crawl into it and get
shot out into space?

Think about it, I say to Big Stick
don't attack me like some deadshit virus.

I'm just going off to see Pick Up
who also has a double life

and might have had his way
with the moon-goddess.

What is the nature of my son's gift?
With much of the way ahead of him

is he giving me a chance
to be my best self?

## Love At Every Turn

Han Shan liked to laugh at the moon
when he did not ignore it.
When he faced it
he wept, before turning his back on it.

This way, that way
he said to himself, as if it mattered.
From time to time
he kept a straight face.

Way back, I met the moon for real
in Marin County, California, the day after
I read The Way of Zen.

It silvered me all night—
woke me, and woke me again
as I sprawled on a redwood deck.

I was travelling alone.
Love at every turn. Promiscuous sweat
stained the Indian turquoise pendant.

Recently, I found it in a gloomy drawer
as if some whacked-out moon
goddess had stowed it away.

One night I'll wear it again.
Along with this new wedding ring.
Never too late to remove a stain.

## Eating Our Words

A damned liar—that handsome son of mine.
He should be a poet.

It was not my idea, he confesses, of the new telescope.
It was the moon goddess, the one you married.

Thank you very much, Nightingale.
What will you do for your next trick?

Such an enviably altruistic man
warrants a name change (if not Nightingale, Boddhisattva).

Last year, as the Plague set in
he gives his flat over to his sister

books specialists for his parlous, ageing mother
he shops for his mother, and for his sister.

Thank goodness for the paramour he loves
and who loves him, and is in residence

in the house into which he has brought
an old friend, a poet who cannot swallow

his food, who in crisis is disabled
by the eating of words.

Goes to show we are all in this together
I say. Nightingale frowns upon my dark side.

And this is how the 'New Year' begins
as we look back into the Plague

and forward to the never-ending wars.
Forgive me, son, I have straw dogs on the brain!

But last night, at the end of a lockdown evening
my wife and I found Billy Holiday alive, on *YouTube.*

Carmine and the open mouth.
Gardenia for the springy hair, her voice indigo

breaking for beauty in sorrow to share—
her singing indigo through and through.

## Near The Ocean

Assembly of telescope pending.

Anyway, it's overcast today.

Our ring-cycle is pending:
this evening
a table has been set at the quay.

All we'll have to do
is look into each other
as roundedly as full moons

with the sound of those first vows
lapping our ears as we
bare throat to bare throat

slipping into the sea of promise
as heart-felt as mother-of-pearl
in scallops of time & salty water.

That's the promise.
The promise of the promise.
That's the spirit of the daffy re-giving

a ring when you have had no ring
and a ring for her when she has.
In their handlings

the rings tinkle like two bells
Han Shan rang in his cave—
ringings that occupied openings.

## After Ritual

Han Shan came home with a band of light
on his finger, the one next to the little one.
A new look for his left hand.

He observed the silver contained darkness also.
A hard luminous thing in moon-shadow.
The newly united made an offering to the evening star.

None of this made Han Shan feel re-wed.
He was as he was and ever had been in himself.
Not much new to say. The silver was white gold and content.

What if he climbed to the top of Cold Mountain
and, under a full moon, tossed the gleam down
cascading cliffs? Happiness soft as water.

## Moon Slightly Behind Cloud

Fancy calling my son Nightingale!
I meant no harm.

Nor did I wish to advance anything womanly:
all I needed to say was Bodhisattva.

My son is not a chip off the old block!
No Way.

As for me: it has to be said
Cold Mountain is a figure of speech.

A conceit.
The make-believe of me being Han Shan—

is an Orientalism
a delirious slip of the tongue—

a dumpling.
Yesterday, a neighbor asked

how I will deal with another year of Plague?
I cleared my throat and went inside.

I wish I could find that damaged copy
of my first Han Shan.

Back then, Watson-san told me
he liked my poems to turnips in Kyoto.

And just recently someone sent me the link
to Cold Mountain on *YouTube.*

There was Burton, lean and tanned, drawling beautifully
tending his diamond prose on a rail of beans.

I should plant more in today's wet soil.
Dad, there's nothing to forgive.

You think so, son, you think so?

## In Sickness And In Health

The contagious in the dusty world
congregate like gulls

inviting rabid dogs
to run among them.

Big Stick and Pickup
are well out of the way.

Big Stick and Pickup—
monk and kitchen hand

know what they want
in silence, in commune

with their co-morbidities.
All they know is the cold

mountain alone as the moon
the one we can see.

They store their food
mendicant and grateful—

rationing words, cleaning up
stray thoughts

holding to tactile conclusions.
It's no good thinking

they believe in love.
It's loving kindness, at best.

Way up, Han Shan listens
to the stars self-creating:

no need for a map, no need at all.
What fool handed me this moon chart?

The telescope still lies dead in its box.
What am I afraid of?

## Sadness

Han Shan could not quite get rid of it—
anymore than me the sea.

No amount of ocean makes us clean
or happy, if it comes to that. Sadness

remains like the sand below.
It's not that it lacks salt, or whatnot

it's not our lack of protection when wet
behind the ears, or anywhere else.

The sea is a kind of clock.
Kind sea, kind time—if only.

On the pier: fisherman with plastic buckets.
The fish swollen, waiting for their guts

to be tossed back into the sea.
Squid spend ink to dry on the planks—

tragic calligraphy; the character for Poem
is Word beside Temple.

Still, water remains the softest reminder
of the ends we meet. Mist was revered by Han Shan.

## Courage To Pick Up

Han Shan must have had the guts
to tough out the thought that
there's little to see, all things considered
on the far side of the moon.

Chinese water, maybe, celestial lakes
of one kind or the other
poets flying high after their shamanic tales
—all that fancy non-sense.

Big birds, and bigger fish
heading off into heroic galaxies
immortal black holes
the paradise of dark matter.

The marvelous list of unknowing goes on.
Somehow, Han Shan, in his mastery
of the laconic, with his slow depth
his powers of acceptance of comorbidities

has it sussed pure and simple.
Burton said he did his best to avoid
*common-taries.* He let the bones
and the best sweet flesh stand.

I imagine I could drink all night
with Burton and Han Shan.
We'd flake out on the deck
and wake with the sun blazing

and think it the one un-abating, splitting
headache we were meant to share.
Maybe that's all I'm meaning to do right here?
Yep, waiting for a Bodhisattva to call.

## Same, Same—

The sizzling
of a wonky white egg
its bottom edge
dripping into darkness

the rest of it a pearl
so white it must have swallowed
its shell, the penumbra
free as a cosmic breeze.

You see it clearly.
She is beside you clearly.
You share regard
reach for each other.

It is what marriage is:
moon-rise with penumbra—
pale grey trace
a footprint

can barely be looked at
defeats the eye, hisses
loss of focus
until swallowed.

## Right Conduct

Out on the reef
swimming over the indigo
and looking down with the ease of moon-viewing
there they are going slow-mo
like birds gliding on thermals—
the butterfish are climbing along cliffs of kelp
their mouths open.

How many circles can you see
without teeth in them, how wide can a moon be?
The fat butterfish is not especially nice eating.
Too soft where it counts
too watery, which is a hell of a lack
for a moon-loving fish.

Yet the skin diver hails the reef fish.
He, or Shaman-she has-moon viewing tact.
The rubbery ones come out of the sea
light as feathers in their lead belts
a modest catch glistening along the spears
where bright virtue runs deep.

## Treading On Dry Kelp

Hey Han Shan
come over here and see this.
Bring Shaman-She with you.

You will need her to count
the untallied bodies in the nets
the fisherman are hauling up.

They have cooled now, the bodies
The pyres made the iron
of the grates melt.

Before that, when living
they were packed onto the long trains
from slums to the sea

carriage after carriage
alive with the plague
everybody breathing

everybody else's
being caste aside:
post Cold Mountain, Han Shan—

nowhere clean to go
to retreat to
to wall up in the Open World.

I've said much against words.
We're heading into the second winter now.
So much scum on the beach

after the storms
after all that I have said
often hardly meaning to speak.

My loves lies ill at home.
Together we are caste, caste.
I can't breathe the way I want to breathe.

What if swimming won't do, Han Shan?
Where to deposit the poem?
What caste reads these days?
What tests to pass, treading on dry kelp?

Han Shan, you arsehole
don't pretend to disappear again
up your mountain into white clouds

leaving me at Sandy Cliff
where anything can happen
with lightning and storms, full moons.

# 3 Dark Pearl

*Human life is less than a hundred years*
*but is weighed down with the grief of a thousand*

*No sooner have you cured a sickness of your own*
*than your loved ones load you with care.*

*Stoop—to see how your grain grows.*
*Look up—see the tips of mulberries.*

*When your counterweight plonks*
*to the bottom of the Eastern sea*
*only then will you have a moment to rest.*

HAN SHAN

## Wave

*I am a Wave Official of the Eastern Sea*
Chuang Tzu

**1**
This is the wave
I seek to name
the one that breaks beyond my reach.

I have seen it rise
year after year
storm after storm, and then some.

It is out beyond the pier
just inside the Rip
that gash in the tide

over the deep.
Its body wide, like a whale
it slides into the bay

from the Strait
breaking into a crest
that flaunts in the sun

and can be seen
in the dark.

**2**
I would not catch that
wave in a fit

but the thought of its
free-fall

does wonders for
the heart.

O for the days.
And I do remember

looking far down
and dropping off the back

to tread water
for the next big one

when I could
make the offering
of myself.

**3**

From the top I kick-started
and nose

dived into sky
water whiteness

down into bumpy air
until I bottomed out

a shoal of foam
behind me.

Han Shan, I imagine
never tired of walking

the long way
up the mountain.

I went straight back out
swimming and diving

like a cormorant
in foam to the

huge silent swell
where waves gathered themselves

listing ultramarine
in green-blue cradling troughs—

Such happy indigo buoyancy
I could not hear a thing until

I looked down a face
up came the alpine roar

there was nothing to it
but the avalanche of self

and a roaring
when there is no self

as it falls
into forms

undoing themselves.

**4**

Forgive this crassness:
today I own the wave.
A photograph of it hangs on the wall.

In the south corner of the studio
it abuts an image of shifting sands—
a dot-painting by a black woman far inland.
I won't promise she's from Utopia, but she probably is.

How the wave got to be beside her
is anybody's guess, ultimately.
Except to say that her sands
are fellow travellers, Han Shan.

They move in their own right.
Each to their own power
and undulating virtue

demanding attention
as a way of life.

**5**

Since it arrived
I have been drawing and painting the wave.
The desert has not come into it.

All I have drawn, so far
is the sliding shelf of the heave
beyond the long pier

the shelter at the end of which
gets busted by storms, lands
as a wreck on the beach.

In reverence, I sketch the wave
a pitter-patter heart in my chest
holding my breath

at the shoulder of the wave
the dark dip
in the throat of its curl

its underside
indigo alive to mind
as paused as a wave at its peak.

**6**

Many a day I work at the wave
sculpturing the foam
before it pours down

its original face. As two
solitary figures at the pier
watch the drama unfold

the wave is time & again single.
I draw only their outlines
leaving them ghostly.

**7**

With a stick of charcoal I drew the couple.
They stood out against the wave.
Smudge the carbon, and they wash into the sea.

The wave, so powerfully still, remains
caught in its movement of solitariness and alas.
Then it races down & across

breaks and is breaking
always with its white crest or breast
of a distant, fully oceanic wave rising up, taking off!

Listen up Han Shan & I'll stop.
I'm just spouting from the shoreline.
Maybe pumped by that painter in Utopia.

**8**

What else?
Of course, there it was again
only yesterday

deeply below me
in a cloud.
Was it a scale-weight

shifting under the sand?
I was a wave passing
over it

then the barb
of its tail was visible:
and to it I was wave-shadow

or a predator born of wave—
hard to know what
most alarmed what.

I am not joking.
Yesterday was cloudy and cold.
Swimming is reaching an end.

The summer has no heat in it.
The sea does not warm.
The fires did not return.

The great ray just signaled
the weight of things
in a time of plague.

## Silver Spontaneity

Still, truth be told, we have yet to assemble the telescope.
Everything remains close up, and filthy:
the scum on the shore break is heavy
from storms, and the aqua is not where it should be
for butterfish and salmon and Mother Ray.
The clear water is on hold, like confounded vaccines.

I have a dreadful fear that recent swims could be my last.
What do they fear the most, the philosophers?
That is the question we should ask a philosopher:
said randy Iris Murdoch, sitting on the filthy knee
of Elias, and Canetti stood up, shook her off
to write a fresh chapter of *Auto da Fe*—

that burning of the books, texts without a Dao.
Words can lose their way without prompting.
Words can float around in the shallows.
Words offer themselves to the gulls, and whatnot.
A word stuck in the gullet is proof of falsity.
Words offering truth get washed out.

Round and round I tread water.
Who said Han Shan could not swim?
Pickup or Big Stick? What a joke.
I am bobbingly quiet as I try to finish this book
in good faith. There is no first person in the vast grey sea.
Like Ding the cook, I slash away

for the sake of *silver spontaneity.*
Flying fish I have yet to see, let alone catch.
They must belong to No-Mind fishing—
as beyond me as wide blue waters, ultramarine
turquoise running into indigo, dark enigma O
indigo let me amble, or dog paddle, like Han Shan.

## Dark Pearl

This morning a second rosella was joined by a third.
If it required intensive care
would it be there?

If I swim today there'll be gulls
and dogs running after them in despair.
At low tide hard sand tests Achilles heels.

The hardships here are neither here nor there.
Someone says nurses are the same all over.
I say I wish each nurse to be a shaman.

I heard a man on the radio, an Australian, a nurse:
he came back here and went back there—
returning to his fiancé, and to the care

involved in being many for others
in doing what he'd been trained to do.
He spoke of his oddity of impulse.

I wonder if he's intimate with Old Walt
returning from the field hospitals?
Old Walt with the lachrymose tongue

Old Walt who loved his citizens to death…
I'm afraid, this morning, of the cold.
Again, at low tide, it will lap lap all too gently.

One swims alone, one loves alone, one dies alone.
The broadcaster set the nurse aright:
not oddity, she murmured, nobility.

Who knows, tomorrow she may not show
in the studio—she'll find another vocation.
As for myself—well, enough said.

Imagine: our listening and hearing
bends with time—its dark pearl of infinity.
Today I want no more news to speak of.

## Days Are Young

Yet again—too late for the firm sand.
Gait plodding, feet sinking.

The tide's almost in, and the waves that broke
quick-time as they rushed towards the empty beach

have slowed in the weary foam of mass-production
and the movement, such as it is, is the dun green

of an abandoned rifle-range, backwash creeks
with nothing doing, which exist between broadcasts

of sound as a surly hiss of negation. To get it all fresh
I'll have to get dressed in the dark

do everything forever the doctor says to do.
I'd have to be down there at dawn

be striding out onto the wide sand
the blazing sun rising in the full breath of me—

*for me!* Fat chance. Ok, I told my wife last night,
I'll put money on fat chance.

(Obesity's a technical term anyway).
And I told her what I had seen only recently

a true morning when I was feeling champ enough
and the shore break had force, I saw

a sturdy—no, a heavy young woman diving
under each wave, presenting her shoulders and torso

to the waves, going over and under and between white rollers
always coming up as pleasant surprise, dolphin wise.

The sea running off her as she stood appraising
The rip near her running sideways fast.

Any minute, I felt, she could be swept away

but her launching and return place was constant
securely in place, or more so than her top:

for a moment there, her breasts were free
and she tucked them in as she went under again.

By then she had been joined by a friend.
(Days when there were women everywhere!)

A taller woman in indigo bathers, also bouncy
and close to the shore as they laughed

and dived under waves together, calling out
to one another, making up for everything.

## This Is The Thing

The last swim I care
to remember for this year

now the lockdown's over haha
as we bare our teeth for the fight

over jabs (cruel diction is
contagous during plagues)

and for the Satanic year before it
when fire came down to the water's edge—

is that I entered the sea so freshened by antibiotics
I swam like a Thorpy

one arm in Prussian blue
the other in aqua

the length of my torpedo
running parallel to submarine

sand sloping into reef indigo
deeper than me deep—

night all the way down and south
to the Antarctic. Hallelujah.

At the edge of darkness—
a glimpse of Baby Ray before

night proper, so help me
and the gods of White Pointers.

I knew it and they knew it!
Unborn, unborn, unborn…

This was the most crystal of outings!
Fit for a shaman, if not me.

You think I just wanted to go south?
Ah, you *think* too much.

## For Too Long

Trying to place
the right words
beside a temple.

Now he totters
putting on his
pyjamas.

He sees the cats
his beloved wife
gently observing him.

Today he must
tell them that
only yesterday

the waste-water truck
came to pump
shit from the storm

water drain.
Vistas of swimming
suffered somewhat!

But next day
he nearly swam the old
full distance

like a man
who'd caught his wave
name or no name.

## Unborn

Has little to do with anything.
It's not original, either.
It's nothing you can point to.

What presses itself upon you
when, surfacing from sleep
you are cold all over?

Days when the rattle
in your lungs is such
your one desire is.

A dog coughs
in the night. Is it
paddling to or from the buoy?

I listen to my wife.
She is hearing me.
O bright, bright days!

As with bright, bright virtue
each hears the other
being unborn.

In the cold sea
piss is warm.
Remember the child born.

You remember everything.
You remember her suffering.
You held slippery sodden arrivals.

A mother gives birth
to a koan.
You are dumbstruck.

And not all of this is true.
Unborn is not entirely the case.
Unborn is sea-shanty.

## Life Boat Shed

How they return, these cormorants
swooping like missiles over the darkening sea
some in a wide arc, others directly on target
each to its roost for white breast, black nape
and evening coat ceremonially folded
as they settle under the eves.

It's happening all year, homecomings all round.
Once upon a time they were sentinels
to the brightly hulled boat inside;
they would have huddled along their beams
in indigo until the alarm bell rang
and the hardy life-saving men arrived

to release the painted boat
at such a speed, with life/death gravity
that it hit the water
with the splash of a whole flock diving.
This is where I sit at dusk in winter
as still as can be, admiring.

At dawn—pale apricot and pink
a mother-of-peal wash in sky and sea.
And the light was a gift for the pastel
gallahs that perched on the roof
and have left already—
well ahead of merciless nightfall.

## Wetsuit

The ocean has come in for its winter.
She enters into it like a seal in summer.

Her return is erect, swift in the shallows
slows when she is thigh-deep.

She is made for love, and is beyond Biblical.
Then she was gone.

As if her muzzle took hold of her progress
her single flipper doing the work of two.

She went at a clip, cutting a swathe, high-finned
setting herself up in the green waters.

I watched her for as far as I could
along the way of the black stonewall.

Where exactly in the chop she slipped out of sight
I could not say. I took my ease

on the walking path, straightening
my back awhile on the hard bench

and only saw her again when
she was almost upon me, her hair loosened

from its rubber cap, her cheeks flushed
her feet bare, the one flipper swinging

to the squelch in her wetsuit.
He feet, tender/tough, braved the bitumen

and we smiled at each other as she passed.
From behind, her legs, wrapped in rubber

were slightly bandy, her bottom ample.
The nape of her neck was olive.

Then I remembered (though I doubt she did me)
her face at the Christmas Eve pulpit.

She'd been asked to read that poem.
And, as I recall, she could only apologize

for her speechlessness since the arrival
of her new-born. My radiance, she seemed

to be saying from the orb she was in that evening
must be allowed, bless us all.

A good swim? I managed speech as she passed.
It's *always* a good swim, she replied, like a sing-song girl.

I walk the black stonewall, hoping to see the day
when her little fucklings follow her into kind waters.

## Fucking Great

When the Indian summer came back
I ran in so furiously as to splash down
flying dolphin-wise over the first break

to breast-stroke underwater
as far as I amorously could
with a soft glide to surface, then

hard on an overarm arc
towards the orange buoy
as far out as my young days.

The surf skis get out there to turn around.
So does the regular squad in their wetsuits
women included, everyone

with shaman powers
for the new year. Proud I am
to recall butterfly kicks

but today the crawl will do.
Not so long back, remember, you were given a medal
for long swims.

They made you a member
of the *Shark Club*
the medal could be read by anyone

who paused at the kitchen dresser
looking for a bottle opener.
Lungs bursting— it was like coming!

Thunder, the Ching says.
Thunder over Water.
Fantastic shit!

The Superior Man
of Dark Learning.
Sages all—anyone, everyone.

## Winter

Today I would have given
almost anything (everything)
to have been out there with them
as distant as the horizon
then swimming all the way in
along the blackstone wall

to land at the summer corner of the beach
—burly magical Yin in late middle age—
having joyfully survived the cold
their breasts and throats warm all the way
only to cry out, as they peeled off masks
and loosened straps: *Oh, Oh, men in black!*

No, they were sardonic, I must say that.
Whatever the Eros, it hit a dry note
for the flock of young tradies at quarantine ease
on the rocks—logoed t-shirts, emptied lunch boxes;
they were soaking up the winter sun
as if they'd never had mothers.

Anyway, I bet, if they'd had their boogies
they'd have paddled past all shaman
signs of origin, behaving as I just did
arriving in the far corner of our garden
where my beloved, in convalescent fever
which was more than a fever

was silently invisibly swimming
about the fire of leaves in her brazier.
Armfuls of autumn smoked her soul
and I could see her essence become
a silver droplet on the tip of her nose.
Her brow was hot, her happy cheeks too wet to touch.

That was enough, and I withdrew.
By now, her sisters who had come in from the cold
would be settled into themselves also.
And the boys they passed on the rocks
would be drinking to their silver roofing.
And the tide would be out again, close to freezing.

## The Way To Go

The less you think the more the water will take you in.

You won't believe the ease of the sea when you give yourself over.

No love has opened to you as ocean has or

given as much to you as courage-heaving sea.

Ever been naked standing in inky, still waters at night?

Or been aroused for exchange, first thing, as the sun makes itself felt?

Grand is the way water deceives by blinding on entry, only

to rinse perception for the wide view of the sea in the arms of the sky.

The birds spot all this as they wheel and cry out above you

while below, the fish are insouciant in the ancestral element.

Some say butterfish do not feel a thing, but even the shortest swim

touches the heart with you don't know what. What happens

when you stroke, caress, fondle sentient beings behind the ears

or if you could, ever so gently, tickle gills?

Feathering vents, as one, as one.

Imagine: swimming from bronze season to bronze season

in all weathers of the ocean that is your garden at Sandy Cliff:

Look! no rubber-ducky protection, may daggy wetsuits perish!

In the depths of sleepless nights, dream Nautilus, and so forth.

*My mind is like an autumn moon*
*shining clear and clear in the green pool.*

*No, that's not a good comparison.*
*Tell me, how shall I explain?*

HAN SHAN

## Notes (you don't need to know any of this)

The Han Shan poems used here are mainly based on the translations of Burton Watson (1970), who I befriended in the last years of his life in Tokyo. Tinkerings were enabled by the versions of Robert Hendricks (1990), Bill Porter (2000), Peter Levitt and Kazuaki Tanahashi (2018). Han Shan (Mountain Cold), the mountain poet of Chinese letters, lived as reclusively as a monk, (or even a shaman), self-sufficiently and in all weathers, descending sometimes to a Buddhist temple, with its kitchen and bathhouse. Legend has it that he wrote poems on walls and rocks and cliffs, as well as using traditional calligraphry materials. Most sources locate his life in the 8th century of the Tang Dynasty.

The Taoism and Zen which informs Han Shan's poems is rooted in the cryptic writings of Lao Tzu's *Dao Te Ching* and the longer, elaborately philosophical, *Chuang Tzu*. Phrases from the former are scattered through this book, such as 'dark virtue', 'straw dogs', 'dark learning'. 'Absolute roaming' is the title of the opening chapter of the *Chuang Tzu*, which is launched with the tale of a phoenix and a giant fish. The limits of thought, and the status of spontaneity in a cosmos of freedom, is the refrain of each book, philosophically/poetically speaking, along with the fluid dance life does with death. I have used various translations, often falling back on the work of my friend, Dr Ian Johnston, translator extraordinaire of early Chinese classics, who lives across the waters from here, on Bruny Island in Tasmania. Its 3rd and final part is called 'The cold light of day' which begins: 'My fall was broken by a straw mattress and I came to no harm.' I plan to read the book after the next swimming season.

The poems in this book arise from two summers of swimming out from The Springs, the beach between Point Lonsdale and Queenscliff. The summer after the fires of 2019-20, at the onset of the plague, while immersed in the above texts, I kept a diary structured by the daily event of entering the sea.

*A Night of Serious Drinking* by Rene Daumal, the title of which arrests me, even as it still lies unread on my desk. It first appeared in France in 1938; Daumal was one of a brilliant group of amusing, surrealist writers concerned with the power of words and the frailty of thought. Its 3rd and final part is called 'The cold light of day' which begins: 'My fall was broken by a straw mattress and I came to no harm.' I plan to read the book after the next swimming season.

*Say it Now*
'Chew on it as hard/as a skull to rest/your sleeping head upon' alludes to the legend of Chuang Tzu who slept with his head on a human skull.

*Survival*
'...We are damned because we do not', Brecht, *Song of my mother.*
*8th Psalm.*

*Watering*
'Petrichor', a song on the 2019 album *Yabby Catcher* by Rose Bygrave.

*Hopeless Moon Viewing*
*Big Stick* and *Pickup*, were Han Shan's off-siders, so to speak; the slap-stick pals, rascals in laughter, buffoons in the antics of poetry. Just as Han Shan could be thought to be Manjushri, the bodhisattva of wisdom reincarnated, *Big Stick* (Shide) was the bodhisattva Samantabhadra. Pickup (Shit-te), was found as an abandoned child by Han Shan, who left him to be brought up at the Kuoching Temple and where he worked and wrote his poems in the kitchen. A poem by Pickup goes:

Cold Mountain is a cold mountain
And Pickup was picked up
Big Stick knows our faces
Fools can't recognize us
They don't see us when we met

When they look we aren't there
If you wonder what's the reason
It's the power of doing nothing.
*The Collected Songs of Cold Mountain.* Trans. Red Pine (Bill Porter)

*Wave*
The wave photograph in my studio, taken by the local photographer, Rodney Nicholson, also hangs in the fish and chip shop in Hesse Street, Queenscliff. The other wave I live with is from the *Kangaroo* series painted by Garry Shead in 1992. In Shead's *The Wave,* the figure akin to DH Lawrence is in disarray and adrift in the 'gaping womb of the sea', along with his naked wife, Frieda. (The phrase is Sasha Grishin's in his *Gary Shead: The DH Lawrence paintings*).

*Unborn—*
resolved a fundamental problem for the Japanese Zen Master Bankei: after years of pondering what a Confucian teacher (on the recommendation of his mother) brought to his attention in the *Great Learning:* that 'the way of great learning lies in clarifying bright virtue". Thus Benkei's way to the Buddhist notion of 'original face'—what might be sought in ourselves, and in each other.

*Wetsuit*
'Sing-song girls' are a lingering presence in some early Han Shan poems as indicated in Robert G. Henricks's annotated translations, *The Poetry of Han Shan*

*Fucking Great*
'The Superior Man of Dark Learning', a common expression for the exemplary sage in the *I-Ching.* 'The Dark Learning' usually referred to the two other ancient Taoist texts, the *Tao Te Ching*, and the *Chuang Tzu.*

# Aknowledgements

This is my second book for Arcadia, and my thanks go to its generous owner, Nick Walker, along with his able staff, including Anna Nechkina, who turned her attention to the final edit.

These poems are published for the first time. The collection owes most to Paul Kane who cast his friendly and fine eye over everything in the first net of this book. During the swimming seasons, the usual flock of friends were subjected to various drafts, helping to keep my spirits afloat: Graham Bird, Lauren Eddy, Rai Gaita, Jennifer Harrison, Phillip Huggins, Jenny Kemp, Richard Murphet, Rod Moss, Ian Roberts, Robert Rosenbaum, Gerry Simpson, Kynan Sutherland, Richard Tanter and Ian Wedde.

My son, Joe Hill, another patient reader, also designed the book. And my wife, Rose Bygrave, brought, yet again, all her intelligent love to bear.

BARRY HILL has worked as a journalist and psychologist in Melbourne and London. He has been writing full-time since 1976 and is the author of many works in several genres, including a libretto performed in 'The Studio' at the Sydney Opera House in 2004. He has written widely for radio, and his short fiction has been frequently anthologized. He's had residencies in Alice Springs, Rome, Kyoto and Santiniketan, Bengal, and is possibly best known for his major works *Broken Song* (Knopf 2002) and *Peacemongers* (UQP 2014). He is a former Education Editor of *The Age*, Poetry Editor of *The Australian,* and a Post-Doctoral Fellow from the University of Melbourne. He lives in Queenscliff, near the Heads of Port Phillip Bay, looking out across the sea towards Tasmania and the Antarctic. He expects his next book to be called *The Tao on Cloudy Bay*. He is married to the singer/songwriter Rose Bygrave.

Printed in Australia
AUHW021156110122
358062AU00008B/22

9 781922 669254